Magnificat

A Devotional

Henry Holt and Company
New York

✦ *Magnificat* ✦

The angel Gabriel
was sent from God
unto a city of Galilee,
named Nazareth,
To a virgin espoused to a man
whose name was Joseph,
of the house of David;
and the virgin's name was Mary.

nd the angel came in
unto her, and said,

Hail, thou that art highly favoured,

the Lord is with thee:

blessed art thou among women.

And when she saw him,
she was troubled
at his saying, and cast in her mind
what manner of salutation
this should be.

And the angel said unto her,
Fear not, Mary: for thou hast found
favour with God.

nd, behold, thou shalt
conceive in thy womb,
and bring forth a son,
and shalt call his name Jesus.

He shall be great,
and shall be called
the Son of the Highest:
and the Lord God shall give unto him
the throne of his father David:

And he shall reign over the house
of Jacob for ever; and of his kingdom
there shall be no end.

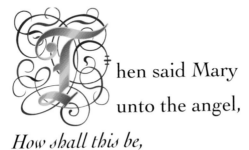

hen said Mary
unto the angel,

How shall this be,

seeing I know not a man?

nd the angel answered and said unto her,

The Holy Ghost shall come upon thee, and the power of the Highest shall overshadow thee: therefore also that holy thing which shall be born of thee shall be called the Son of God.

And, behold,

thy cousin Elisabeth,

she hath also conceived a son

in her old age:

and this is the sixth month with her,

who was called barren.

For with God

nothing shall be impossible.

 nd Mary said, *Behold the handmaid of the Lord; be it unto me according to thy word.* And the angel departed from her.

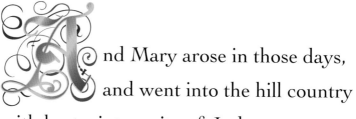

nd Mary arose in those days, and went into the hill country with haste, into a city of Juda;

And entered into the house of Zacharias, and saluted Elisabeth.

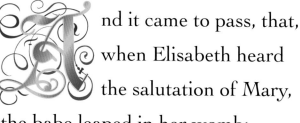 nd it came to pass, that, when Elisabeth heard the salutation of Mary, the babe leaped in her womb; and Elisabeth was filled with the Holy Ghost:

And she spake out
with a loud voice,
and said,
Blessed art thou among women,
and blessed is the fruit of thy womb.

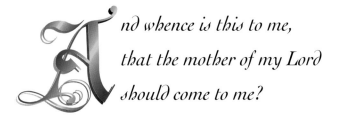

nd whence is this to me,
that the mother of my Lord
should come to me?

For, lo, as soon as the voice of thy salutation sounded in mine ears, the babe leaped in my womb for joy.

And blessed is she that believed:
for there shall be a performance

of those things which were told her
from the Lord.

nd Mary said,
*My soul doth
magnify the Lord,*

*And my spirit hath rejoiced in
God my Saviour.*

For he hath regarded the low estate of his handmaiden: for, behold, from henceforth all generations shall call me blessed.

For he that is mighty
hath done to me great things;
and holy is his name.

And his mercy is on them that fear him
from generation to generation.

41

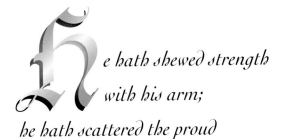

he hath shewed strength
with his arm;
he hath scattered the proud
in the imagination of their hearts.

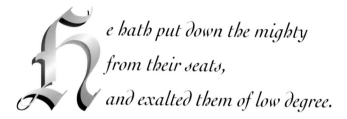

He hath put down the mighty
from their seats,
and exalted them of low degree.

He hath filled the hungry with good things;
and the rich he hath sent empty away.

e hath holpen
his servant Israel,
in remembrance of his mercy;

As he spake to our fathers,
to Abraham, and to his seed for ever.

The Paintings

⊹ Rogier van der Weyden ⊹
The Annunciation

Considering that Rogier van der Weyden is generally thought of as the leading Netherlandish painter of the mid-fifteenth century, it is ironic that so little is known for certain about him. During his lifetime, his work was greatly admired and emulated both north and south of the Alps, and he had a large, active workshop that kept his tradition and spirit vital for decades after his death.

The Annunciation is a fine example of this master's painting. It demonstrates Rogier's ability to achieve a remarkable clarity of color and line in his works. True to its Northern origins, it is freighted with symbolic detail. The Virgin's purity is alluded to by the lily in a vase, the clear bottle of water on the mantle, and the golden ewer on the bedstand. While the setting — Mary's bedchamber — and her position seated on the floor point to her humility, the richness of the setting and Gabriel's robes suggest Mary's future role as Queen of Heaven.

Rogier van der Weyden, Netherlandish, 1399/1400–64
The Annunciation
Oil on panel, 33 1/2 × 36 1/4 in. (86 × 93 cm)
Louvre, Paris (inv. no. 1982)
(Details on pages 2, 16, and 19)
Photograph: © PHOTO R.M.N.

Sandro Botticelli, Florentine, 1445–1510
The Annunciation
Tempera on panel, 58 1/2 × 61 13/16 in. (150 × 156 cm)
Uffizi Gallery, Florence (inv. 1890; no. 1608)
(Details on pages 8, 9, and 13)
Photograph: Erich Lessing/Art Resource, NY

✣ Sandro Botticelli ✣
The Annunciation

At the peak of his career, Botticelli was the most popular artist in all Florence. He painted some of the most renowned and important commissions of the time, including portions of the Vatican's Sistine Chapel and numerous works for the Medici family, among them his two best-known — *Primavera* and *The Birth of Venus*. By the time of his death, however, he had been eclipsed by Leonardo da Vinci. He died in relative obscurity, which lasted until the Pre-Raphaelites revived interest in his art in late nineteenth-century England.

The Annunciation was painted during the 1480s, a time when Botticelli, along with many of his fellow Florentines, was held in thrall by the preaching and charismatic mysticism of the Dominican Savonarola. As a result of the monk's stern teachings, the sweet, often sentimental and decorative beauty associated with Botticelli's earlier works was replaced with a tendency toward dramatic gesture and a severity in the execution of detail and landscape.

Giovanni Battista Cima da Conegliano, Venetian, 1459/60–1517/18
The Annunciation, 1495
Tempera and oil on canvas, transferred from panel,
53 1/4 × 41 3/4 in. (136.5 × 107 cm)
The Hermitage, St. Petersburg (inv. no. 256)
(Details on pages 10 and 24–25)

✢ Cima da Conegliano ✢
The Annunciation

As his name attests, Cima was born in Conegliano, a small town near Venice. He moved to the city of canals during his youth and it was there that he created most of his paintings. Cima's *oeuvre* is marked by beautiful evocations of Venetian interiors and northern Italian landscape. His style reveals a strong influence of the Venetian master Giovanni Bellini.

Cima's ideas about the Annunciation also reveal a knowledge of painting from the Netherlands. This may be seen in his choice of the Virgin's bedchamber as the venue of the picture, much as Rogier van der Weyden did for his *Annunciation* (see page 53). Traditionally Venice welcomed Jews who wished to live there, and their influence may be seen in the Hebrew inscription on the bedstead — the Old Testament prophecy of the virgin birth. The simplicity of the room, contrasted with its situation high enough to afford a spectacular vista of a city on a hill, may refer at once to the Virgin's humility and to her placement on high.

✦ Carlo Crivelli ✦
The Annunciation, with St. Emidius

Carlo Crivelli was born in Venice, where he developed his considerable talents as a painter. He later moved to a town in present-day Yugoslavia before settling finally in the Italian region known as the Marches. He seemingly confined his artistic output to the painting of religious images, of which this painting is among the greatest and best known. Crivelli was a master at rendering elaborate scenes with complex perspectival schemes, overlayed with elegant, finely detailed decorative surfaces.

The Annunciation, with St. Emidius was an altarpiece painted for a monastery church in Ascoli Piceno in northern Italy. It places the sacred event of the Annunciation in the midst of everyday happenings, its only witnesses being the child at the left and a young man toward the back, both of whom glimpse the flash of light as the Holy Spirit descends. Accompanying Gabriel is the town's patron saint, Emidius, who carries a model of the city under his protection.

Carlo Crivelli, Venetian, ca. 1430–93
The Annunciation, with St. Emidius, 1486
Egg tempera on canvas, transferred from panel,
80 3/4 × 57 1/8 in. (207 × 146.5 cm)
National Gallery, London (NG 739)
(Details on pages 1, 15, 23, and 41)

✣ Nicolas Vleughels ✣
The Visitation

The eighteenth-century Parisian painter Nicolas Vleughels was active just a generation before François Boucher and Jean-Honoré Fragonard, but his elegant Baroque style is rooted in a period and approach that are several steps away from the Rococo confections of the later painters.

Placing his holy figures in a contemporary setting and dress, Vleughels charged his scene of the meeting of the Virgin and St. Elizabeth with a relevant, persuasive dramatic element. The bright blues and yellows of the angel-laden heaven contrast brilliantly with the warm tones of the earthbound setting, making it clear that this is the moment when the older woman feels her unborn child stir within her, revealing that she is in the presence of the Mother of the Savior. The Virgin's demeanor betrays little comprehension of her role, even though she stands on the threshold of an understanding that will prompt her to exclaim "My soul doth magnify the Lord."

Nicolas Vleughels, French, 1668/69–1737
The Visitation, ca. 1729
Oil on panel, 13 7/8 × 10 5/16 in. (35.5 × 26.5 cm)
The Hermitage, St. Petersburg (inv. no. 1888)
(Details on pages 20, 31, and 32)

✢ Studio of the Master of 1518 ✢
The Visitation of the Virgin to St. Elizabeth

In the nineteenth century, art historians devised a way of "naming" anonymous artists, particularly those of the Netherlandish school. By giving works to "masters," who usually received names based on specific works or on styles associated with them, many previously unattributed paintings neatly developed authors.

The Master of 1518 was an anonymous painter who has been given credit for many beautiful works created in Antwerp in the early sixteenth century. His name comes from an altarpiece in Lübeck that is dated 1518.

This *Visitation* from the master's studio is a tender evocation of the event. Particularly important is the attention the painter paid to specific details of Luke's narrative while setting the scene in a contemporary Flemish landscape. The depiction of Elizabeth as an elderly woman is especially apt. Artists often took the license to show her as being of an age closer to that of Mary.

Studio of the Master of 1518, Netherlandish, early 16th century
The Visitation of the Virgin to St. Elizabeth, ca. 1515
Oil on panel, 31 3/16 × 27 1/8 in. (80 × 69.5 cm)
National Gallery, London (NG 1082)
(Details on pages 26–27)

✣ Mariotto Albertinelli ✣
The Visitation

As a student in Florence, Mariotto Albertinelli befriended his fellow student, Bartolommeo Baccio della Porta. The latter's fascination with the ideas preached by Savonarola led him to give up painting temporarily and enter a Dominican monastery. Now known as Fra Bartolommeo, this monk's painting is among the greatest of Florentine Renaissance religious art. Albertinelli, whose small *oeuvre* reveals a leaning toward monumental figures and classical settings similar to Bartolommeo's, tired of the criticism artists face and gave up painting to become an innkeeper.

The Visitation is one of his masterpieces. His placement of Mary and Elizabeth before a majestic classical arch bestows a monumentality on the figures befitting their symbolic roles. But it is their intimate greeting that reveals the humanity of the holy women. Combined, these elements suggest the spiritual import of the birth of John the Baptist —and, ultimately, of Jesus Christ— foretold by this image.

Mariotto Albertinelli, Florentine, 1474–1515
The Visitation, 1503
Oil on panel, 90 1/2 × 56 15/16 in. (232 × 146 cm)
Uffizi Gallery, Florence (inv. 1890; no. 1587)
(Detail on page 29)
Photograph: Scala/Art Resource, NY

✤ Titian ✤
The Annunciation

Titian was one of the few Renaissance painters to achieve and maintain tremendous success throughout his long lifetime. But more remarkable is the fact that this admiration has never paled over the course of the centuries since his death. *The Annunciation,* one of his finest paintings, has recently been dated to around 1522, when the artist was in his mid-thirties.

The symphonic composition, the bounding energy of the angel, who hovers in midair, and the tranquil piety of the Virgin all contribute to the exquisite beauty of the painting, but the secret of the intimacy and warmth of this enormous canvas lies in the care with which Titian rendered even the smallest details, such as the Marian symbols—the guinea fowl, the sewing basket, and the apple. The delineation of the tile floor draws our eye to the landscape-like tumult in the background, which stands in for the agitation that must have disrupted Mary's unearthly calm.

Titian, Venetian, ca. 1490–1576
The Annunciation, ca. 1522
Oil on canvas, 67 3/4 × 103 3/4 in. (166 × 266 cm)
Scuola Grande di San Rocco, Venice
(Details on pages 35, 37, and 38)
Photograph: O. Böhm, Venice/IKONA

✦ Jan Brueghel the Elder ✦
The Adoration of the Kings

Jan Brueghel the Elder, sometimes called "Velvet" Brueghel
due to his ability to render exquisite textures, was the son
of the Netherlandish master Pieter Bruegel. He is best
known for his flower paintings and his brightly colored,
intricately constructed landscapes. Much of his technique
with the latter is evident in this remarkable small work.

The psychological complexity of this *Adoration of the
Kings* just begins with the variety of style of dress and
architecture. While the picture is brimful with figures in
northern dress of the sixteenth-century, the central figures
of the drama wear costumes more in the tradition of
religious painting. Brueghel has brilliantly composed this
complex image, permitting glimpses of life beyond the
manger. Though the world remains unaware of what is
unfolding just around the corner, there can be no question
as to the magnitude of the event that comprises the primary
focus of this image.

Jan Brueghel the Elder, Flemish, 1568–1625
The Adoration of the Kings, 1598
Bodycolor on vellum, 12 13/16 × 18 3/4 in. (32.9 × 48 cm)
(Details on pages 42 and 48–49)
National Gallery, London (NG 3547)

⚜ Juan de Flandes ⚜
The Nativity

As his name implies, Juan de Flandes was born in Flanders, but he made his reputation in Spain. Along with numerous other Netherlandish painters, Queen Isabella brought him to the Spanish court in Castile, where he was ultimately elevated to the position of court painter in 1498.

Juan de Flandes's exquisite miniaturistic style is revealed in the few works of his that survive. *The Nativity* is from an altarpiece. It displays a wealth of detail but does not feel crowded or overdone. The artist used a popular means of telling a complicated story with a minimum of elements: the Adoration of the Child is knitted together with the Annunciation to the Shepherds by the gaze of Joseph, who witnesses from his post in the manger the message of the faraway angel. Here, the owl is an attribute of Christ, who comes to "give light to them that sit in darkness." That Mary's robe is black rather than the more usual blue may be a nod to the painter's Spanish patrons.

Juan de Flandes, Hispano-Flemish, active 1496–1519
The Nativity, ca. 1508/19
Oil on panel, 43 1/2 × 31 1/4 (110.5 × 79.3 cm)
Samuel H. Kress Collection, National Gallery of Art,
Washington, D.C. (1961.9.23.(1383)/PA)
(Details on pages 45 and 46)
© 1995 Board of Trustees, National Gallery of Art

Henry Holt and Company, Inc.
Publishers since 1866
115 West 18th Street
New York, New York 10011

Henry Holt® is a registered trademark of
Henry Holt and Company, Inc.

Published in Canada by Fitzhenry & Whiteside Ltd.,
195 Allstate Parkway, Markham, Ontario L3R 4T8.

Library of Congress Catalog Card Number: 95-80846

ISBN 0-8050-4649-6

Henry Holt books are available for special promotions and
premiums. For details contact: Director, Special Markets.

First Henry Holt Edition — 1996

Designed by Peter M. Blaiwas

Printed in Singapore
All first editions are printed on acid-free paper. ∞

10 9 8 7 6 5 4 3 2 1